FIVE
5
FINGER
PIANO

Over the Rainbow
and Other Great Songs

ISBN 978-1-4768-1292-2

CORPORATION

7777 W. BLUEMOUND RD. P.O. BOX 13819 MILWAUKEE, WI 53213

Visit Hal Leonard Online at
www.halleonard.com

Chitty Chitty Bang Bang

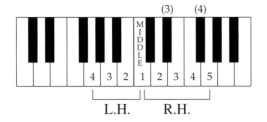

Words and Music by Richard M. Sherman
and Robert B. Sherman

Brightly

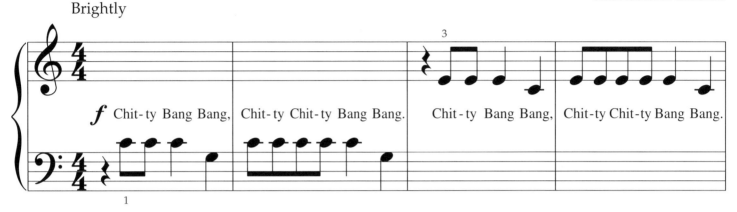

f Chit-ty Bang Bang, Chit-ty Chit-ty Bang Bang. Chit-ty Bang Bang, Chit-ty Chit-ty Bang Bang.

Chit-ty Bang Bang, Chit-ty Chit-ty Bang Bang! Oh, you, pret-ty chit-ty bang bang,

Duet Part (Student plays one octave higher than written.)

Bright

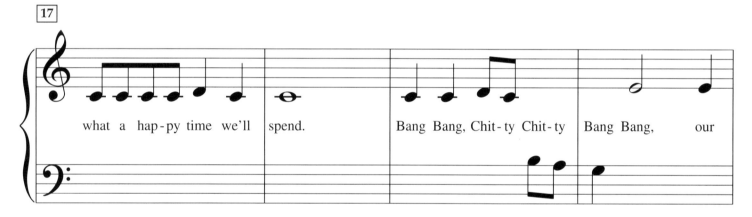

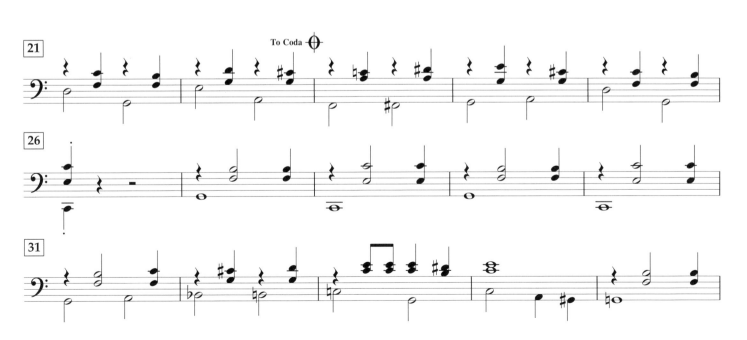

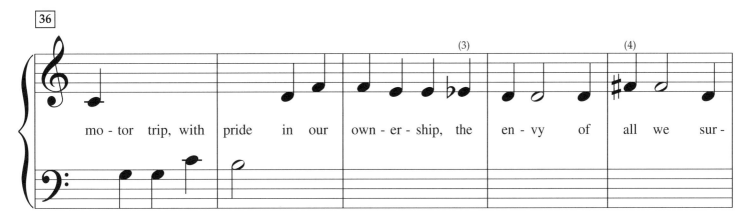

mo - tor trip, with pride in our own - er - ship, the en - vy of all we sur -

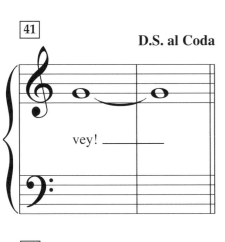

D.S. al Coda

vey! _____

CODA

Bang Bang, Chit - ty Chit - ty Bang Bang, our fine four -

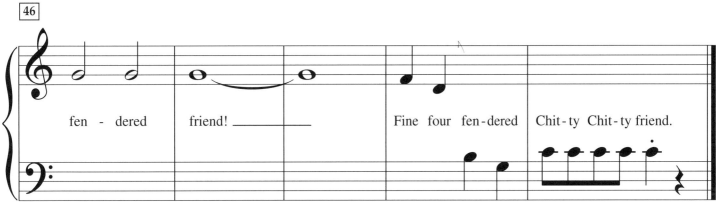

fen - dered friend! _____ Fine four fen - dered Chit - ty Chit - ty friend.

Ding-Dong! The Witch Is Dead

from THE WIZARD OF OZ

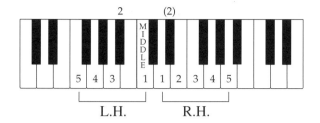

Lyric by E.Y. Harburg
Music by Harold Arlen

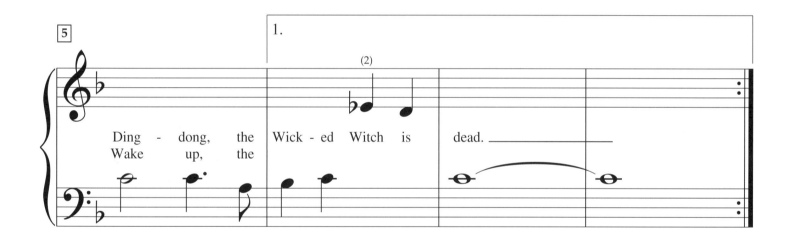

Duet Part (Student plays one octave higher than written.)

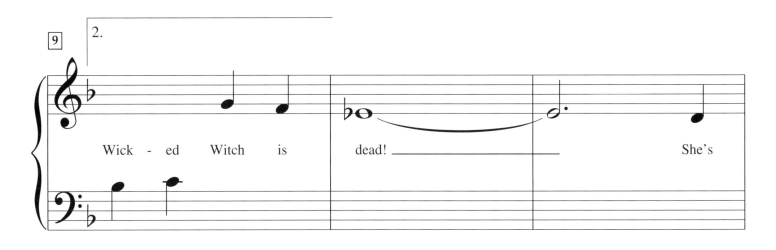

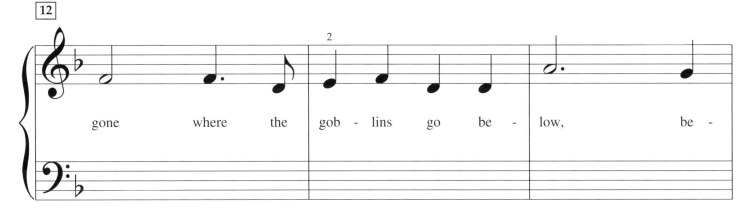

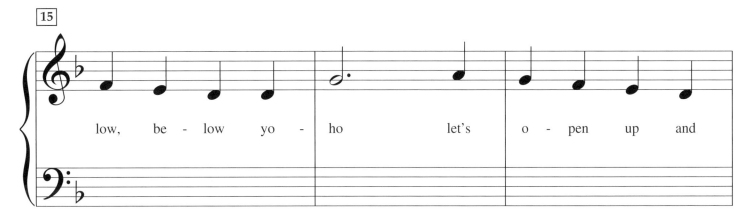

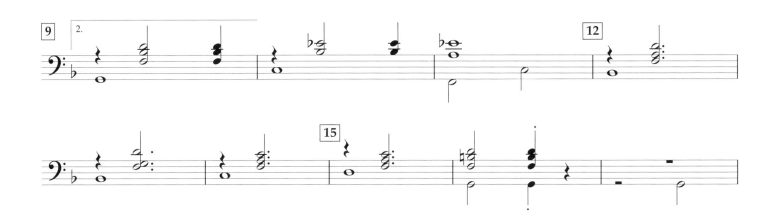

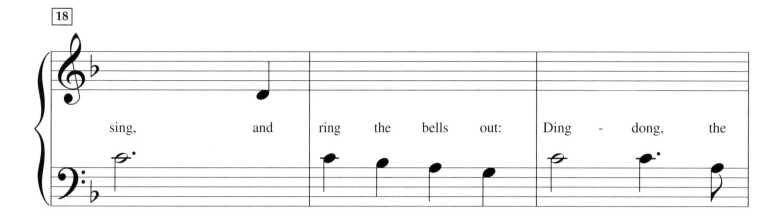

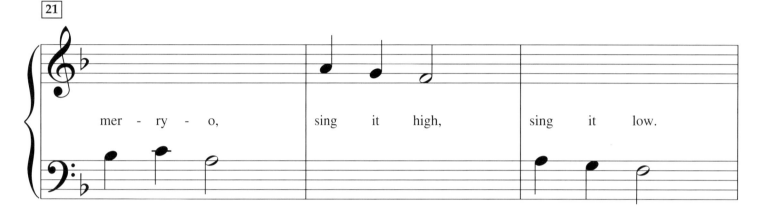

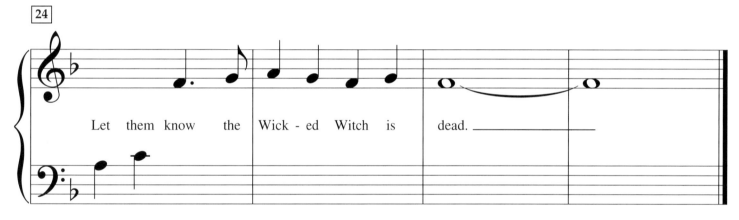

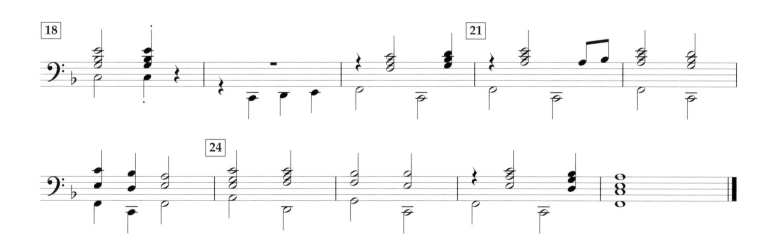

Over the Rainbow
from The Wizard of Oz

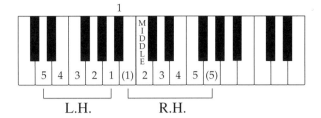

Music by Harold Arlen
Lyric by E.Y. "Yip" Harburg

Moderately slow

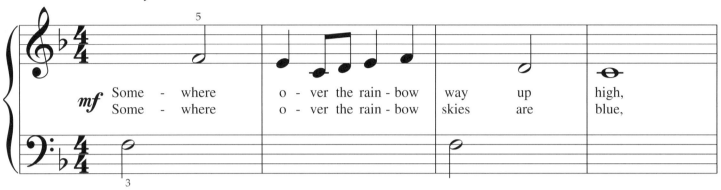

mf Some - where o - ver the rain - bow way up high,
Some - where o - ver the rain - bow skies are blue,

there's a land that I heard of once in a lull - a - by.
and the dreams that you dare to dream real - ly do come

Duet Part (Student plays one octave higher than written.)

Moderately slow

mp
With pedal

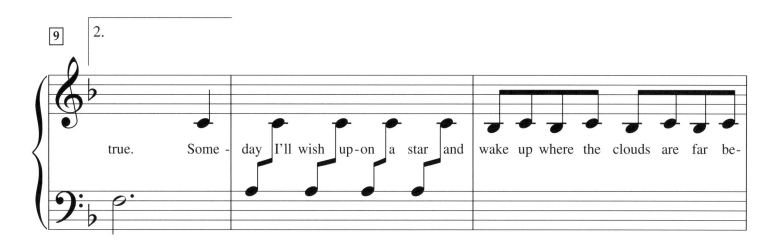

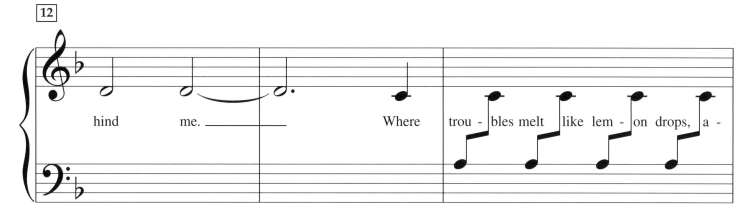

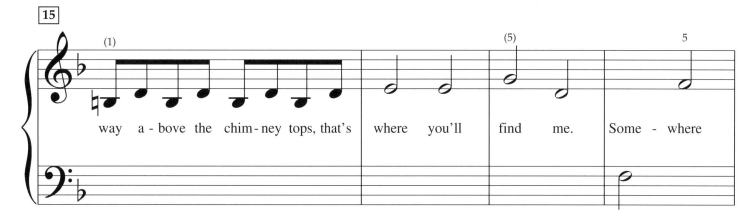

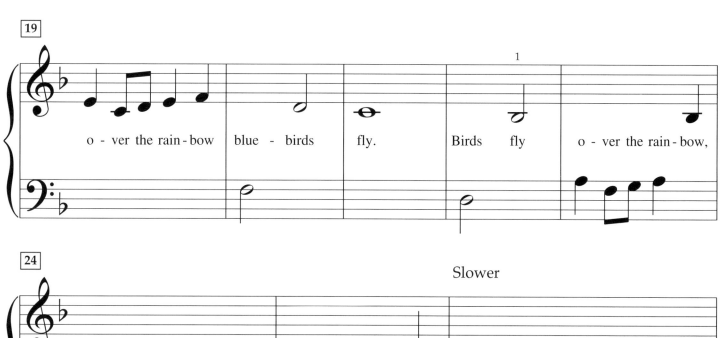

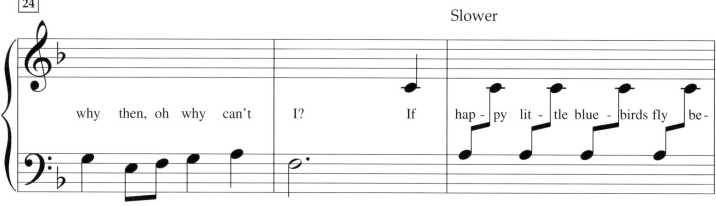

Good Night

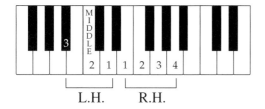

Words and Music by John Lennon
and Paul McCartney

Sweetly, dreamily

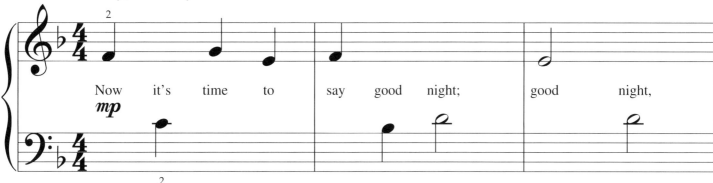

Now it's time to say good night; good night,

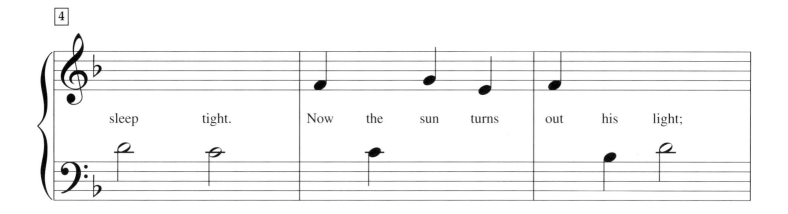

sleep tight. Now the sun turns out his light;

Duet Part (Student plays one octave higher than written.)

Sweetly, dreamily

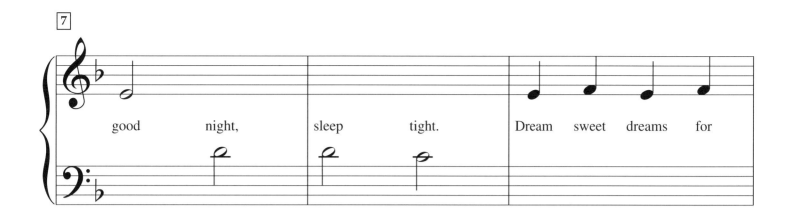

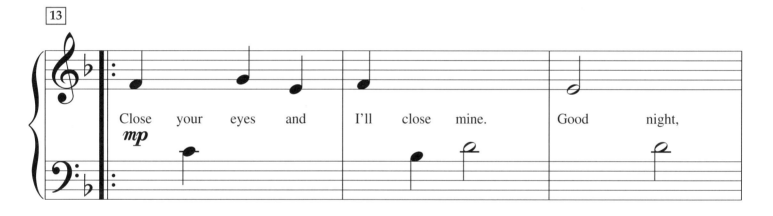

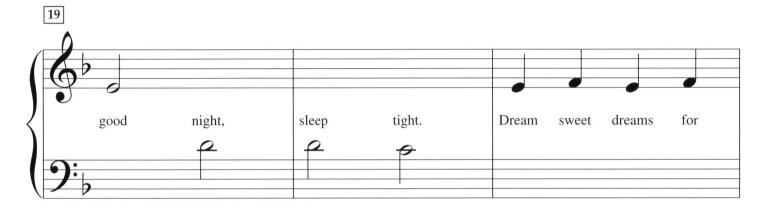

Mm ——— mm ——— mm. ———

p

(Whispered:) Good night,

good night everybody, everywhere everywhere, good night.

rit.

pp

pp

rit.

ppp

Goofus

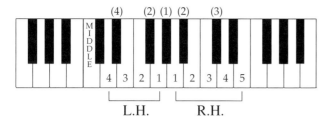

Music by Wayne King and William Harold
Words by Gus Kahn

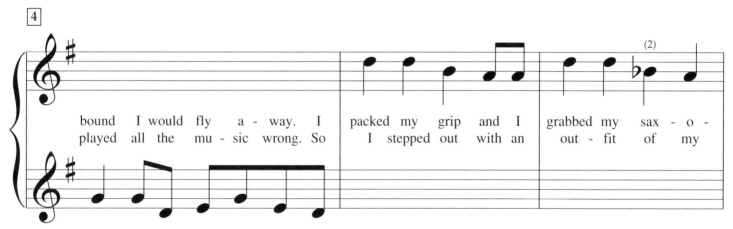

Duet Part (Student plays as written.)

The Hokey Pokey

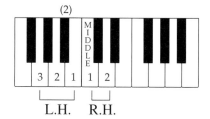

Words and Music by Charles P. Macak,
Tafft Baker and Larry LaPrise

Moderately

You put your *right foot in, you put your *right foot out. You put your *right foot in, and you
2.–10. *(See additional lyrics)*

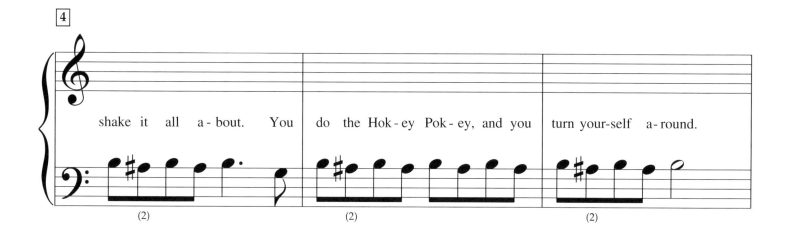

shake it all a-bout. You do the Hok-ey Pok-ey, and you turn your-self a-round.

Duet Part (Student plays one octave higher than written.)

Moderately

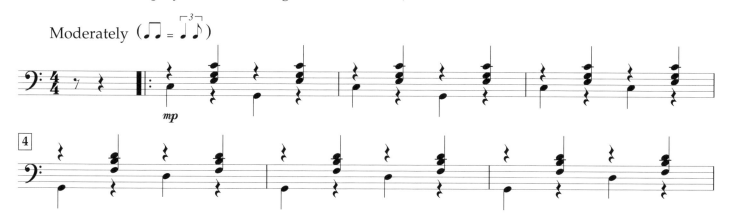

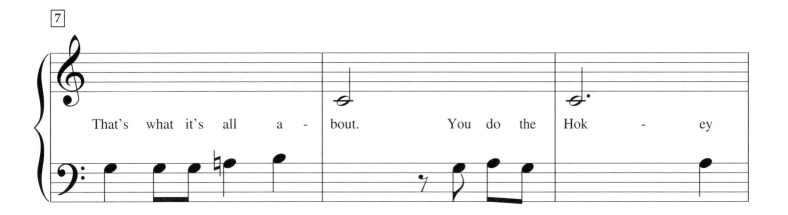

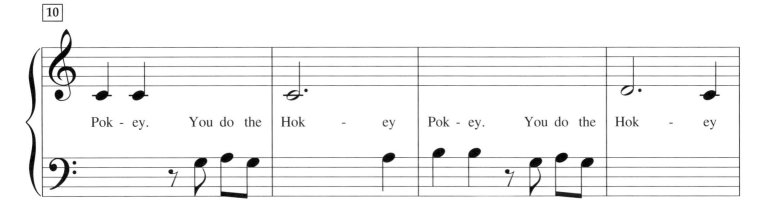

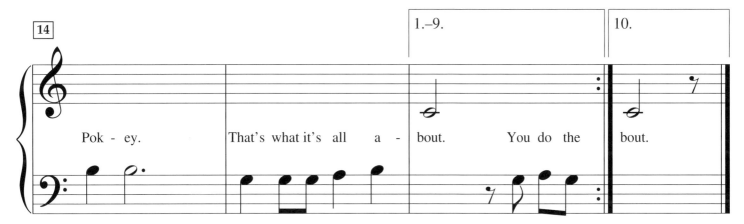

Additional Lyrics

*2nd time: left foot   *3rd time: right arm   *4th time: left arm
*5th time: right elbow   *6th time: left elbow   *7th time: head
*8th time: right hip   *9th time: left hip   *10th time: whole self

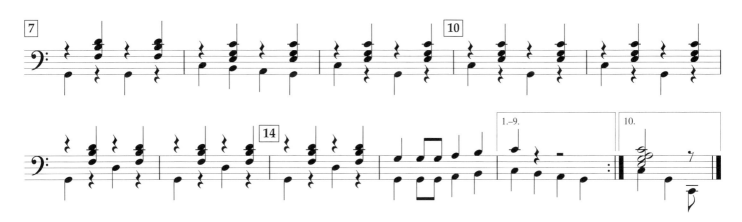

I'm an Old Cowhand
(From the Rio Grande)

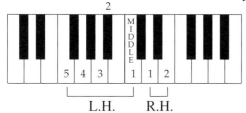

Words and Music by
Johnny Mercer

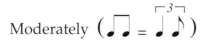

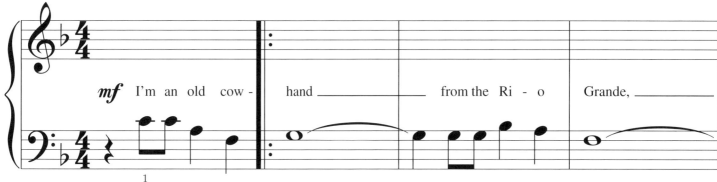

Lyrics:

I'm an old cowhand _____ from the Ri - o Grande, _____

but my legs ain't bowed _____ and my cheeks ain't tanned. _____
and I learned to ride _____ 'fore I learned to stand. _____
and I come to town _____ just to hear the band. _____
where the West is wild _____ 'round the Bor - der - land. _____

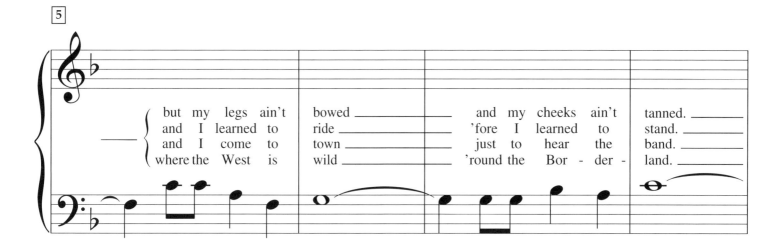

Duet Part (Student plays one octave higher than written.)

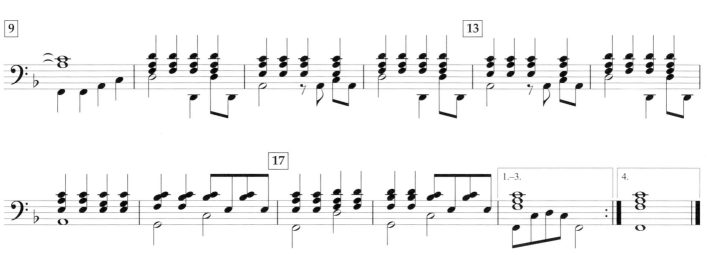

The River Seine
(La Seine)

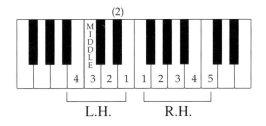

Words and Music by Allan Roberts
and Alan Holt
Original French Text by Flavien Monod
and Guy LaFarge

Moving along

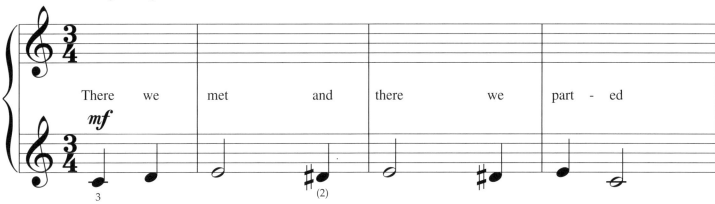

There we met and there we part - ed

mf

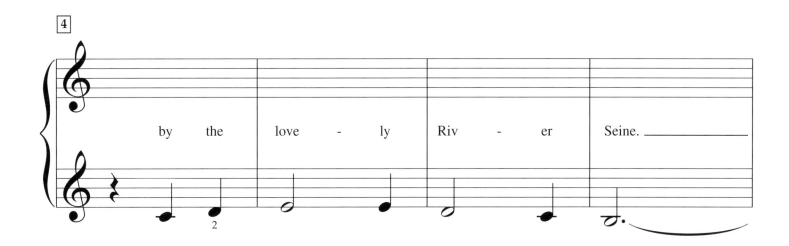

by the love - ly Riv - er Seine. _____

Duet Part (Student plays one octave higher than written.)

Moving along

mp
With pedal

Splish Splash

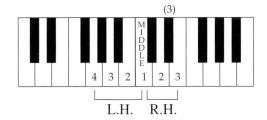

Words and Music by Bobby Darin
and Murray Kaufman

Rockin'

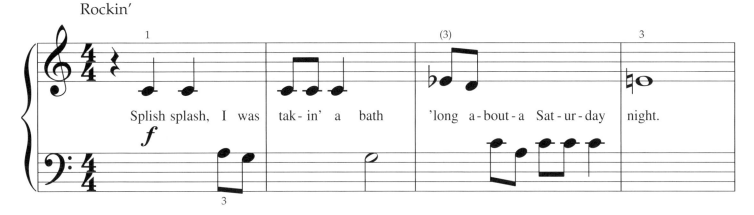

Splish splash, I was tak-in' a bath 'long a-bout-a Sat-ur-day night.

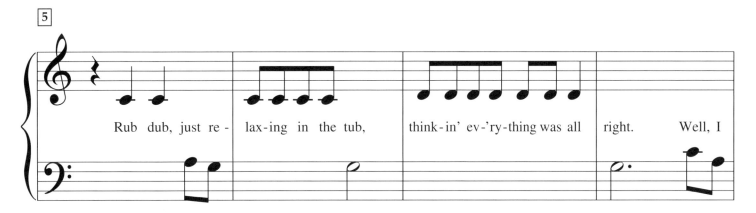

Rub dub, just re-lax-ing in the tub, think-in' ev-'ry-thing was all right. Well, I

Duet Part (Student plays one octave higher than written.)

Rockin'

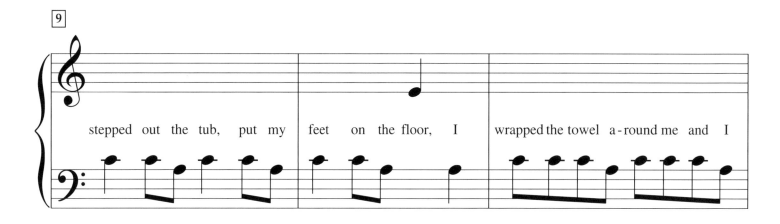

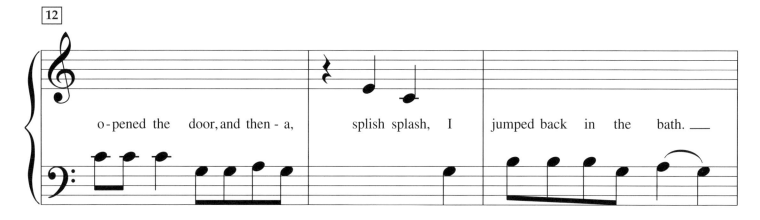

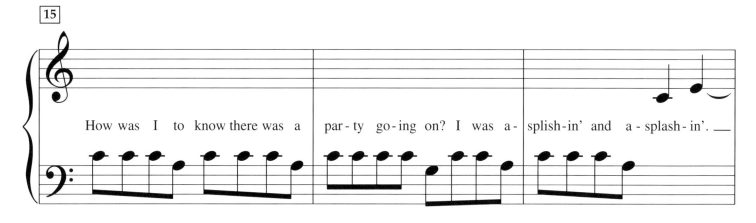

Additional Lyrics

Bing bang, I saw the whole gang, dancin' on my livin' room rug.
Flip flop, they were doin' the bop. All the teens had the dancin' bug.
There was Lollipop with Peggy Sue. Good golly, Miss Molly was-a even there, too.
A-well-a, splish splash, I forgot about the bath. I went and put my dancing shoes on.

This Land Is Your Land

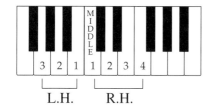

Words and Music by
Woody Guthrie

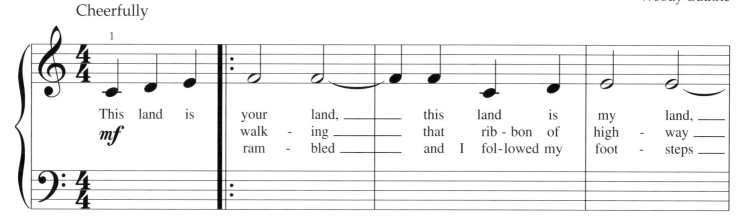

Duet Part (Student plays one octave higher than written.)

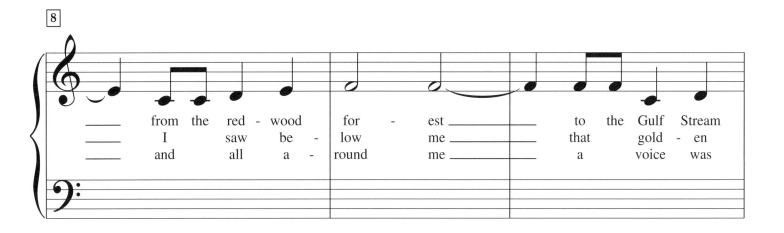

from the red - wood for - est _____ _____ to the Gulf Stream
I saw be - low me _____ _____ that gold - en
and all a - round me _____ _____ a voice was

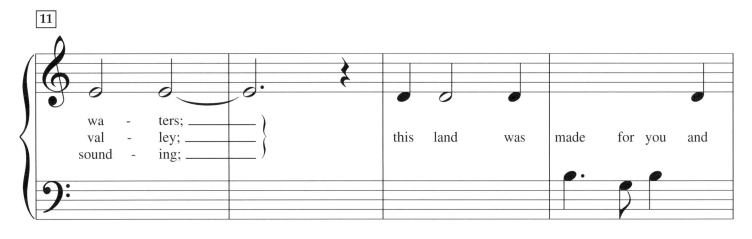

wa - ters; _____ _____
val - ley; _____ _____   this land was made for you and
sound - ing; _____ _____

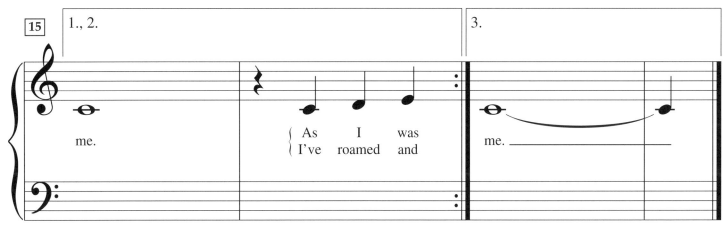

1., 2.

me.

{ As I was
{ I've roamed and

3.

me. _____

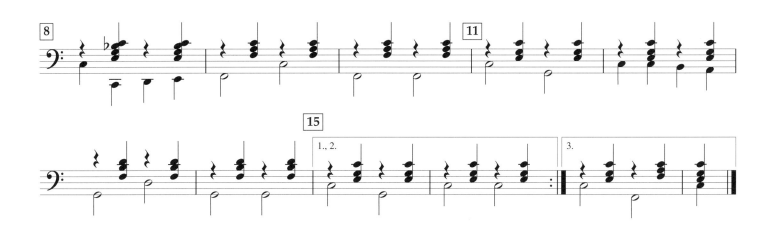

PLAYING PIANO HAS NEVER BEEN EASIER!

FIVE 5 FINGER PIANO

5-FINGER PIANO COLLECTIONS FROM HAL LEONARD

BEATLES! BEATLES!
8 classics, including: A Hard Day's Night • Hey Jude • Love Me Do • P.S. I Love You • Ticket to Ride • Twist and Shout • Yellow Submarine • Yesterday.
_____ 00292061 ....$8.99

CHILDREN'S TV FAVORITES
Themes from 8 Hit Shows
Five-finger arrangements of the themes for: Barney • Bob the Builder • Thomas the Tank Engine • Dragon Tales • PB&J Otter • SpongeBob SquarePants • Rugrats • Dora the Explorer.
_____ 00311208 ....$7.95

CHURCH SONGS FOR KIDS
Features five-finger arrangements of 15 sacred favorites, including: Amazing Grace • The B-I-B-L-E • Down in My Heart • Fairest Lord Jesus • Hallelu, Hallelujah! • I'm in the Lord's Army • Jesus Loves Me • Kum Ba Yah • My God Is So Great, So Strong and So Mighty • Oh, How I Love Jesus • Praise Him, All Ye Little Children • Zacchaeus • and more.
_____ 00310613 ....$7.95

CLASSICAL FAVORITES – 2ND EDITION
arr. Carol Klose
Includes 12 beloved classical pieces from Bach, Bizet, Haydn, Grieg and other great composers: Bridal Chorus • Hallelujah! • He Shall Feed His Flock • Largo • Minuet in G • Morning • Rondeau • Surprise Symphony • To a Wild Rose • Toreador Song.
_____ 00310611 ....$7.95

CONTEMPORARY MOVIE HITS – 2ND EDITION
7 favorite songs from hit films: Go the Distance (Hercules) • My Heart Will Go On (Titanic) • When You Believe (The Prince of Egypt) • You'll Be in My Heart (Tarzan™) • You've Got a Friend in Me (Toy Story and Toy Story II) • more.
_____ 00310687 ....$7.95

DISNEY MOVIE FUN
8 classics, including: Beauty and the Beast • When You Wish Upon a Star • Whistle While You Work • and more.
_____ 00292067 ....$7.95

DISNEY TUNES
Includes: Can You Feel the Love Tonight? • Chim Chim Cher-ee • Go the Distance • It's a Small World • Supercalifragilisticexpialidocious • Under the Sea • You've Got a Friend in Me • Zero to Hero.
_____ 00310375 ....$7.95

SELECTIONS FROM DISNEY'S PRINCESS COLLECTION VOL. 1
7 songs sung by Disney heroines – with a full-color illustration of each! Includes: Colors of the Wind • A Dream Is a Wish Your Heart Makes • I Wonder • Just Around the Riverbend • Part of Your World • Something There • A Whole New World.
_____ 00310847 ....$7.95

EENSY WEENSY SPIDER & OTHER NURSERY RHYME FAVORITES
Includes 11 rhyming tunes kids love: Hickory Dickory Dock • Humpty Dumpty • Hush, Little Baby • Jack and Jill • Little Jack Horner • Mary Had a Little Lamb • Peter, Peter Pumpkin Eater • Pop Goes the Weasel • Tom, Tom, the Piper's Son • more.
_____ 00310465 ....$7.95

GOD BLESS AMERICA®
8 PATRIOTIC AND INSPIRATIONAL SONGS
Features 8 patriotic favorites anyone can play: America, the Beautiful • Battle Hymn of the Republic • God Bless America • My Country, 'Tis of Thee (America) • The Star Spangled Banner • This Is My Country • This Land Is Your Land • You're a Grand Old Flag.
_____ 00310828 ....$7.95

MOVIE MAGIC – 2ND EDITION
Seven gems from the silver screen arranged for beginners. Includes: Chariots of Fire • (Everything I Do) I Do It for You • Heart and Soul • I Will Always Love You • The Rainbow Connection • Summer Nights • Unchained Melody.
_____ 00310261 ....$7.95

THE SOUND OF MUSIC
8 big-note arrangements of popular songs from this perennial favorite musical, including: Climb Ev'ry Mountain • Do-Re-Mi • Edelweiss • The Lonely Goatherd • My Favorite Things • Sixteen Going on Seventeen • So Long, Farewell • The Sound of Music.
_____ 00310249 ....$8.99

HAL•LEONARD® CORPORATION
7777 W. BLUEMOUND RD. P.O. BOX 13819 MILWAUKEE, WI 53213
www.halleonard.com
Disney characters and artwork © Disney Enterprises, Inc.

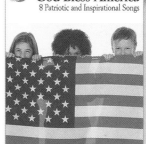